Copper Bones
By Patrick McGinley

Dedicated to:
MyGrandparents who traveled from Ireland to make a life
for us all us Magfhionnghanle's in the New World.
To Riley and Savanna McGinley, my greatest gifts. and
My Brother Kevin, for the stories and the memories. Slan.

Shooting Die.

If a fella has more than twenty one dollar bills in his pocket
there is something nefarious afoot.
The possession of the single note currency is not the preferred
make up of a man's pocket loot.
Tens and fivers do not hold this stigma as they seem a
legitimate amount for cash on hand.
The one dollar bill is the trouble maker of currency and with it
the stories that are far from bland.

The one dollar bill and never the coin are welcomed calling
cards at the bars where women dance.
Mind you this is not a get together of dear friends and the
women present are not seeking romance.
Flat out they want every penny you have and they are as
patient as vultures as they pick you clean.
Making it rain is proof positive at the waste of cash that
ensues feeding the debauchery machine.

It is not this waste of good money for a bad reason that is the
only proof when it comes to the buck.
It is a sure sign there was some gambling was recently done
and possibly losing the title of the truck.
I have gambled in many casinos over my time but I was never
a threat of taking the house down.
It was more like amusement such as taking a roller coaster
ride that you do when the money is found.

Outside the casino's I have seen and taken part in some
private games of both cards and shooting dice.
These games pop up in an afternoon visitation and all hold the
potential to become anything but nice.

Ship, Captain, Crew is a fast moving game using five dice with the goal being to get the highest point.
When one dollar bills start piling high on a Saturday afternoon saloon plank a nose can get out of joint.

The beers and drinks are flowing as the jukebox serenades the atmosphere to gamble up the paycheck.
This is where one can get into serious trouble when the game becomes a place you do not wish to trek.
I have seen some very serious conversations take place next to the bathroom or in another dark corner.
Those are the games I walked away from when I see paychecks being cashed or seeking a cash loaner.

The best story about a game of dice is one I cannot write about but it involved a great deal of cash.
It was held in a men's room where the floors of marble provided the stage to lose his money stash.
It got very ugly as I witnessed with others, the calling in of the I O U right at the end of the game.
The line of credit was allowed with the promise of immediate payment win or lose and with no shame.

It was stated there was no moola available to cover the check the mouth wrote which means a bounce.
This is where it got scary physical as lightening could discharge with the electricity in the air to trounce.
Payment would be collected in a rather unusual manner involving cash and a car being surrendered.
If the deal fell through there was a promise offered to the chap about unconscious being rendered.

I never wake up with a stack of singles crumpled in my pocket
as I piece together earlier activities.
I do play an occasional friendly game of dollar dice as I did on
so many Butte bars over the years.
Some of those simple dollar games brought a bit of excitement
to the bar as side bets kicked in.
If lady luck was on your side a fella could have an evening
paid for including all his heavy drinking.

I hardly recall being in many bars outside of the Mining City
where a game of dice broke out.
You knew a game was underway when you walked into a
Butte bar as the players did shout.
Those roust about games that involved more trash talking
than of a plan to clean out a wallet.
Make up for some of my best times in Butte bars and I'm
grateful to be here on God's earth to tell it.

Kevin's Ski Doo.

Asking if my brother Kevin was up for an adventure was like
asking Hitler if he likes to invade.
Kevin was known for his antics including strapping a green
bird about his waist in the St Paddy's Parade.
Kev left us too early and that is only buffered in the peace we
all had in his passing after the parents.
It is an Irish Blessing that is prayed for by all to go before their
children to wear the Lord's garments.

Being the next in line and the last of the McGinley boy's Kevin
and I hung out more than the others.
There was about three years between us and we enjoyed
many of the same things like good brothers.

One early Sunday Morning Kevin rousted me out of an early
AM sleep to see his new snow machine.
I got up and got dressed good and warm knowing a ride was
on the agenda after my visit to the latrine.

Snowmobiles first became popular when I was just two years
old and then they made it to this place.
The Ski Doo Kevin had purchased was one of the original
apparatus's which he rode with no disgrace.
It had seen better times but ran like sewing machine and it
flew like the wind on the Montana ice.
Kevin decided we should recess to Scoop Bar while inviting
me to ride with him on deaths device.

I straddled on back and told Kevin "Hit it Kato" and in
seconds we were off and making fast tracks.
Not one car was on the roads that morning as I hung on to the
comet while praying and trying to relax.
About of foot of new snow had blanketed Butte as we roared
on to First Street heading to the park.
Kevin hit Hebgen park wide open, a sucker punch to the calm
peaceful Sunday morning just after dark.

We flew through the park in record time and he had so much
fun the first time we turned around.
The blowing through the snow and the sound of the
contraption was sure to awaken all in town.
We made it to the Scoop Bar in three pieces, me the machine
and my brother Mad Dog the musher.
The bar was open and warm as Joe the swamper brought us
antifreeze for the morning to be ushered.

We stayed at the bar for the rest of the morning as the
Breakfast Club showed up for morning mass.
By Noon it became apparent we needed to get the death trap
in the garage as we drank up our last.
One again we mounted the machine and to my surprise Kevin
behaved his ass on the ride back home.
Kevin wrecked the beast weeks later at Georgetown where a
picnic table hid in a snowbank unknown.

I would not dare take a golf cart on my city streets for fear of
getting a ticket or arrested right away.
When we pulled hijinks like the snowmobile ride in Butte the
police gave us more than a little leeway.
The outlook on that Paul Revere morn might have been as
long as no one is hurt we'll give you a break.
Butte allowed you to live a bit more than most others and it is
a life I wish to never replace or retake.

There must be thousands of stories in Butte families regarding
the hay day and antics of the few.
I am not sure if this behavior is celebrated anywhere but to
wild Appalachian Mountains might do.
Butte is a bit clannish and it looks out for the other fella
especially when the limits are pushed.
It is that camaraderie that I miss the most and that I will
always remember times never hushed.

Leo.

I developed an ego when I was doing radio that would put off
people when I was an ass.
When one writes his own press releases and believes his own
lies success will surely pass.
My errors in life were compounded when drinking and I dare
not face the honest truth.
When wrapped in a cocoon of self-deception the shallow
wisdom I had was in a tooth.

I have to be honest these days when looking at my life and I
try to make it the best I can.
That was not the whole story when I was selfishly drinking
until I could no longer stand.
I have put the cork in the bottle and now writing is my vice as
I sort out this hectic world.
I find pleasure in the simpler things such as finding my dog
by the fireplace lying up curled.

Being sober today makes me a far better person and with the
regret I wish I quit earlier.
I realize that this gift of sobriety was always there for me and
that I was the only barrier.
When seeking the guidance to deal with this world it is best to
find a wise caring soul.
It needs to be a person who has lived in the hell of pain and
never once lost self-control.

I visited with Monks in the Carolinas as in my search they
seemed to have what I needed.
After a time the Brothers thought I should return to the world
and that's advice I heeded.

I searched for the answers though I knew not the questions I
needed to address and ask.
When disappointment struck instead of turning to God I
foolishly climbed into the wine flask.

It has been many years since I touched the drink daily but still
I felt empty and wan.
Why am I here and who decides who is worthy after so many
have left and are gone.
It is this quest that brought me full circle as I now find many
of my answers at home.
It is the simple code of living I was raised with in Butte which
is why I write this tome.

The gift of understanding has been given to me from a fellow
who offered assurance.
He was not a priest or a holy man who offered advice he is the
seller of life insurance.
My friend Leo McCarthy is one of those men who sat back
and enjoyed a great life.
He and others were robbed of the life of their angels and here
is the dismissal of strife.

Leo turned a tragedy that would have maimed others and
made a new vision quest.
He took the absence of a daughter's life and turned it into a
giving value for all the rest.
Leo has counseled the worst and stood by the troubled as he
guided their foggy thoughts.
His message to carry on without the need of self-destruction is
the message they sought.

I offer these words for the world to consume as a respectful
message to all of life's hope.
It is the message of Leo to hang in there and to tie a knot when
at the end of life's rope.

Be strong for yourself and you will benefit many others is the simple unselfish proposal.
I am proud to call Butte's Leo McCarthy a best friend and a lifelong guide and a great pal.

Tom.

I was in fourth grade at St Joes and a few of my brothers were enrolled in Butte Central.
The Butte Central tumblers were a major half time show with all boys and not one gal.
The tumblers allowed a few of us young to come and learn how to be a Central tumbler.
We went to the Gym careful not to walk on the schools emblem as we met the Brothers.

We went into the gym and the excitement of being part of the team filled our ambitions.
The idea of jumping and vaulting with the historic team filled our spirits with elation.
As we stood about waiting for our turn a man entered with a flat top and a Maroon shirt.
It was Tom Petrich who we all knew very well he was to Central what the Earth is to dirt.

Tom worked the room giving advice and shaking hands while patting others on the back.
My oldest Brother Mike introduced me to Tom as we watched the human pyramid stack.
Tom waved good bye as he headed out the door to head to watch the football team.
My brother informed me to never make fun of Tom as he was a part of the Central dream.

Tom attended every game that he could and he was welcomed by every player and coach.
His knowledge of team members and their stats was a talent many wish they could poach.
Tom was never once reprimanded and I recall seeing him walking the sidelines at games.
He watched and supported every Central sport with enthusiasm that was hard to tame.

When the Maroons lost a game the student body took the loss with anger and disappointment.
Tom would get upset at the losses but always had a "get them next time" announcement.
After graduation I returned to see some of Buttes games and I seemed to always see Tom.
He seemed ageless to me as he hustled the sidelines ready to drop his applause bomb.

Tom passed away and it has been decades since I have seen him so I do not claim to be close.
The last time I saw him he nodded his recognition to me as he was dressed in Maroon clothes.
Tom lived for Butte Central and was a part of every team that geared up for a Butte Central game.
I am proud to know Tom and he taught us the lesson to dance with person you took to the game.

His dedication to Central was recognized by all the students as he was protected and held high.
If there was any possibility Tom could have participated his enthusiasm would reach the Big Sky.

I understand Tom followed the Maroons for the remainder of his time and was accepted by all.
Tom was a gentleman, and avid Central fan and a team leader who never touched a game ball.

Kardashians need Butte.

I consider myself a gay Irishman, I like women over whiskey.
I believe women are here as a gift to man from the Almighty.
I could write for hours on my appreciation of the weaker sex.
To start I would not call them weak so sit back a bit and relax.

I wrote once how Lindsey Lohan could use some Butte guidance.
In a months' time she would be sober and keeping on her pants.
The lessons I learned growing up in Butte stay with me today.
I also believe that Butte could bring in any Hollywood stray.

The Kardasian tribe is a good example of needing a Butte visit.
In a short time they would turn around their lives of Bullshit.
I would drop Kanye West at Park and Main with ten bucks.
He would realize he is not cool and no one gives two fucks.

Kim and Khloe would be best served to visit Maloney's Bar.
Their crying antics would be called and attitude won't go far.
They need to go more than a day of being in the living class.
Behave in public and for God's sake, cover up that fat ass.

The one who would benefit the most is Kris their Mom.
I would send her to the Reservation to be beaten like a drum.
I would take them all in a car to the Silver Bow home complex.
I'm sure they would find the need for basics not just spandex.

Bruce Jenner I would take him fishing and away from Kim.
He would learn there is more to life than just them and him.
I think a few days of Butte Camp would turn the fools around.
It would be a good lesson to learn of life in the Mining Town.

Butte calls bullshit at the drop of a hat when one is
misbehaving.
I think the Kardashians would realize the need to change, no
hesitating.
I do my best to be as a good citizen as was my Irish Mom and
Dad.
The Kardashians would be better off in life if my parents they
had.

Scars are better than Tattoos.

A few of us guy's had this discussion one time about the
capturing of events on one's skin.
The debate started when we read a shirt that "Scars are better
than tattoos" applied with a pin.
I can look at the scars on my body and I have a story to go
with every one of the violations.
The skin is the biggest human organ and I am amazed at what
it can endure in bad situations.

I have a scar on my shin about six inches long that involved
me wrestling with barbed wire.
I have a half moon crescent on my forehead when I took a
cheap shot from an ass and sad liar.
My left index finger almost got removed by an ax as I
chopped firewood while out camping.
I was in the emergency room so many times they should have
offered frequent visitor stamping.

My five brothers and I kept the emergency room quite busy
with stiches and X-Rays galore.
The visits were part of growing up in Butte and I am sure
many others add to this score.
You may have visited the emergency room to often when a
strange nurse knows your name.
Falling off of roofs and wrecking of cars were adventures
where not one hooligan is to blame.

My Dad was the best guy when it came to getting repaired at
the body shop we called Saint James.
Every one of us boys visited the emergency room more after
an accident with no one feeling shame.
My Dad and Mom showed genuine concern but were the first
to tell us to get up and get moving.
It be casts or stitches involved in the treatment the same
applied as their tough love was forgiving.

As I am sure you can imagine there were some very close calls
especially when we all drank.
It was not just car wrecks involved as there were more than a
few saloon brawls to thank.
Being an all boy fraternity in the name of the Shamrock the
membership seemed very limited.
The fraternity was not only me and my brothers as all the
neighborhood kids were initiated.

Being born in Butte we were not hauled to the hospital for a
bump or simple splinter.
A few times the wounds were to minor and home surgery was
done in the winter.
Large knots on the head might lead to a concussion and
experience kept us awake.
My parents took turns watching the patient with no reason to
visit the ER intake.

To this very day I know there are times I should have visited a Doc for a small wound.
I can carefully apply a butterfly bandage with precision as if a Doctor was around.
Do not take this story as being abusive or that I lacked attention when I was hurt.
If we went to the ER every time one of got injured the parents credit would be dirt.

I am thankful today that I learned to shake of the pain and to how walk off a smack.
The common sense approach my parents displayed for us does not warrant an attack.
Things were different in my day as I am sure they with you as we limped into the future.
I know what is important and how to handle it all even when others think I need a suture.

There is a great analogy about how the hard times in Butte make living later a bit easier.
When one self-evaluates his health and position in life those past lessons are a savior.
I'd be a fool if I thought at times I was not cared for, as my parents did what was best.
I find issues today are much easier to handle as I look back while finishing on my quest.

I know that someone is reading this and saying I live far too much in my Butte mining past.
I will pleasantly disagree with the uniformed fool as those Butte lessons continue to last.
Being from Butte means you were baptized in blood and genuflected on a skinned knee.
Every bump and cut I got and the thumps on my soul are fine thanks to my Butte history.

Growing up on Nevada Street.

I would like to believe that everyone I know had the
furtherance I knew growing up on my street.
We were woven together in the magic carpet time of the
sixties and rock and roll was the beat.
It was a great time to be an Irish kid as John was the Pope and
Kennedy was running the land.
The mines and pits were blasting and roaring and the
Company was creating its destructive brand.

The Labor Department's office was called the
"Unemployment Office" as all seemed to be working
Being an artist for the State and drawing benefits was short
lived but Disability claims were increasing.
There was "Apples" Conrad on the corner who was bent at his
waist after failed surgery on his back.
And Herbert Heard who had the consumption were the only
two who did not work out of the Dad pack.

With a Yahtzee dice difference in ages with my brothers there
were diversified interlopers at the abode.
Doors slamming closed rang throughout the alleys as the Pit
expanded and the East Ridge did erode.
With an industrial playground specked with Iron Pyrite and
Arsenic we dusted off and got back up.
It was the dawn of color television owned by a few who
curled up to watched after the evening sup.

The family haberdasher was JC Penny and we listen to Opie
get life lessons as we lived out our own.
There were no backpacks full of school books and work
buckets sustained Dad's moving ore and stone.

I walked a few blocks to school and The Bluebirds were only
needed for sports and trips in the field.
The three o'clock bell announced the two legged livestock
release and public schools barriers did yield.

It would be decade before we would see the release of the
Walkman and technology did not exist.
Metal Erector Sets lent to the development of imagination and
Hot Wheels kept boy's minds affixed.
Notes were passed to flirts with the girls and text was the
referral to a book used in the classroom.
The fascination of life's engagements was in real time and face
to face living had not met its doom.

I write not these proses for a shameful and wasted indictment
on today and the joys of the flat screen.
I will bitch about the constant staring of a device in everyone's
hands to narcissistically self-preen.
I do not attempt to understand the need of duck lip poses and
the need to twitter what you just ate.
I do waste a wish or two every day requesting a return to the
times when life was of a simpler state.

Aunt Marg's Body and Fender

My Uncle Gab on my Mother's side was a Scotsman and
damn proud of his life's frugal approach.
He made the Buffalo on the Nickel moo from his firm hold on
money which no one could encroach.
In the disposable throw away world of today we toss out
phones and electronics like used tissue.
It can drive one to lunacy when looking at the waste of energy
and money as if it is no big issue.

For those members of large families there were lessons
learned early on the stretching of a buck.
It began with buying clothes to factor in growth spurts and
changing the oil in the car or truck.
Communal societies of the sixties were similar to the large
Butte family far outside of California.
Wardrobes meshed with others and communal closets
maintained the family clothing cornucopia.

The best lessons learned were the ones designed by necessity
and mirrored in our personal desire.
The building of bicycles melding parts of another, too using
spit to find the air leak in the front tire.
I do not recall men farming out a job on their houses
especially when they had hours of free child labor.
Many a roof was attached and trim work painted using the
child work force and an occasional neighbor.

Conveniences and major purchases were weighed out with
special care and given financial discretion.
Purchases were not made to keep up with the Jones's or to
project a move in societal upper direction.

A large project needed attention and it was deemed a sound
investment for the households good.
Options were tossed about in conversations at the kitchen
table weighing out every should or could.

I was raised with ingenuity as if it was a childhood friend
watching over dollars was a lesson learned.
There were no daring undertakings and modifications of how
a large family spends money Dad earned.
Our pants were bought long and a long cuff was tucked under
to respond to six boys growing legs.
Coats could be interchanged as most sweaters with numerous
backups hanging on hallway pegs.

One story involves money and my Aunt Marg who never
knew "No" when a challenge was there.
With her quick mind and keen hands as a Widow she learned
early to fix it or stich it for a repair.
Realizing early she would need the independence of a car her
hard cash was saved and set aside.
Within a short period she was the proud owner of a well
running Volkswagen bug for a daily ride.

There was not one downside of the car for Aunt Marg as it
was dependable and just her size.
It got her up and down the richest hill on earth daily and not
once giving a mechanical surprise.
There was one small set back as far as Marg was concerned
and it was the Bug needed some paint.
Even though it was a small car the price of a professional
spray job raised a small fiscal complaint.

Aunt Marg decided to take the bull by the horns or in this case
to take the bug by the front bumper.
She boldly decided to paint the car herself using small cans of
spray paint sold where she got lumber..

Some men might cringe at the thought of a woman taking
discounted spray cans to the body of the car.
I believe their mind would be at ease if they knew my Aunt
Marg and her great spirit that carried her far.

She purchased a light beige paint that was on sale and
proceeded to mask off the all the cars chrome.
One afternoon she started to paint away in the little garage in
Walkerville underneath the family home.
I am not sure how many cans she used nor do I know how
many hours it took for the entire paint job.
I do know that it looked like a million dollars and the light
beige color stood out in the traffic mob.

The little Bug's paint job did not peal or flake as it lasted
through dozens of Montana's tough winters.
Aunt Marg smiled at the blessing of her little tan bug as it took
her from Walkerville to the city center.
It is that gratitude and problem solving I learned from my
Aunt Marg and all the Irish women I love.
A solution is always at hand as long as you are penny wise
and willing to put on a set of work gloves.

Dandelion Wine with the Hutterites.

If you live anywhere close to the Montana Highline there lays
a group of German folk.
They go by the title of Hutterite and according to them they
carry God's heavy yoke.
With crisp white shirts banded with suspenders and heads
topped with a gold straw hat.
They are materialistic as Donald Trump as they punch out a
rural life off the country fat.

If you know me in anyway personal you would know I have
no strangers in my life.
I can talk the wings off a duck and Christ off the Cross while
causing very little strife.
I met many a Hutterite in the casinos and bars as they sold
their veggies and eggs.
One thing I can tell you is the Hutterites are big drinkers and
make wine by the kegs.

They have one particular blend they call Dandelion wine as
sweet as summer corn.
They carry it by the gallon and will sell you a bottle while
spinning a country yarn.
The broken English they speak is peppered with German and
hard to understand.
All troubles fall aside when talk turns into money ending up
in their farmer's hand.

You can deal with the elders of the tribe but I prefer to find the
way ward young buck.
These are the ones who enjoy getting off of the ranch with
purloined wine in their truck.
They smoke corn cob pipes and are searching for machine
made cigarettes to torch.
They like drinking forbidden whiskey and getting wild when
they are off the family porch.

There is one major issue with the Hutterites and that is getting
women to join the cause.
It is a hard sell living in weather forty below zero giving any
sane woman reason to pause.
The Hutterites are always trying to win over women, like
pimps at a Greyhound bus station.
Most find it easy to turn down the offer realizing being a
Hutterite bride is no vacation.

The women keep close to themselves and dress puritanical including a maid's bonnet.
It is a purpose of the men to keep them tethered to the group in an ever present dragnet.
To me they have the vacant stare of a sniper watching the city life they never will live.
They are clogs in the man-made religious life, asking more than any human should give.

Those born into a weight of life and are forbidden to look at the world beyond a windshield.
Do they climb into bible or do they play a game of mind travel becoming a Barbie doll in a field.
I find truth in the last observation for their Men folk put on their ass hats when at the trough.
The ride home after a visit to the big city was probably as boring as watching the rising of dough.

My interactions with the interlopers occurred for the three years I bounced around the Hi Line.
It is not the end of the world where the Hutterites live but you can see it from there after time.
I have come to the conclusions that like other religious orders their life is not cut out for me.
I also believe that the Hutterites are doomed for extinction if they don't get some new pussy.

Montana Thespian.

Sunday afternoons rekindle a friendship consummated with
beer drinking in Missoula, Montana.
It was not exercised in the bar rooms down town or in any
Biker bars while donning a bandana.
The Sunday services were held in a crack in the wall
apartment on the tough side of the tracks.
It was the apartment of my buddy Billy Powell in a hidden
place where luxury and wealth were lax.

Raised in Avon and sheltered from the winters in his Mothers
one stop bar and full service store.
Billy and his family fractured and were scattered with Billy
ending up in theater doing an encore.
He was married once but she was never discussed as Bill
acknowledged his drinking caused a split.
Bill returned to the Garden city with dreams of hang gliders
being sold and becoming a financial hit.

The hang gliders did make a small mark but Billy abandoned
the enterprise without making a dime.
As with his tripping the light fantastic in the Pasadena
Playhouse his efforts fell short of sublime.
It is just after the return to Mootown that Billy Boy brought his
theatrics and singing out to air.
He became the lounge singer at the German Beer house and
slipped into roles for the theater.

He was a tour guide for visitors to the Garden City as he spun
outrageous stories about local sites.
It did not hurt that he was three sheets when performing his
duty much to his own personal delight.

He was a small part player for the Children's theater company
in fact it was one of his last worldly acts.
I understand he did not touch one drink when rehearsing his
part and avoided his daily six packs.

True to many predictions made by those quick to judge it was
drinking that brought Bill's final bow.
He was hit and killed by a drunk driver as he walked from the
wrap party sober as a Hindu's cow.
Billy got a headline in the Missoulian and a final article
written by an old friend captured his antics.
When one struggles with everyday life and chooses the drink
the results are not boring or pedantic.

Bill was a funny old codger who befriended many in his
journey and is missed by his family.
He never intentionally hurt anyone but sure pissed off more
than a few pushing the insanity.
His family asked the sentencing judge to show the young man
compassion in Billy Boys name.
I know in my heart Bill would have granted a second chance
for the kid to live with no shame.

My days and nights in Bill's garden were full of laughter and
discussions on all under the sun.
I head butted Bill the first day that I met him as I was unaware
his big mouth was meant in fun.
We were good friends up until the final curtain on Bill's life
when it came down that fall night.
I am a bit more tolerant and no longer head butt so I am sure
Bill would think my path is right.

The Aneurism of Grief. 1977

There is a patch in my life that saw the death of friends strung
together on times necklace.
All were lost by the action of their own hand as they hit the
wall in their troubled human race.
These were not quiet exits but explosive moments where one
minute of peace could be a stall.
For some reason I understand completely what they went
through and then again not at all.

All the members of this crew ran together for decades and in
the final stage they hit life hard.
A life style built on bindles of cocaine and waterlogged with
whiskey made them all a wild card.
The docile passing of our souls into God's hands seems to be
the last wish of most folk I know.
That dream like request was not available to these lads
derailed by mountains of white blow.

These were all good men who were a bit wild at times and
walked outside the common law.
What they envisioned in their resolution of the problem was
laced with scenes only they saw.
They chose a path of least resistance for all knew that a
turnaround needed to take place.
Some looked at jail and others total heartbreak but all wanted
to find peace and save face.

Not one day goes by that I am not reminded of their actions to
surrender to the wrong choice.
The problem was there were no ears to listen to each of these
fella's weak and fearful voice.

They felt all alone with their solutions inhaled from a mirror and searched for in an empty glass.
I know firsthand of that despair experienced and the shame of deeds when you can't get a pass.

I know in my heart that each had to regret their actions as all would like to be part of each day.
Their action of panic in a moment of turmoil could have found the solution if you are willing to pay.
It is selfish by some and sad for others but no matter the opinion there is one resounding truth.
Give the worst of times the grace to pass you by and find joy while getting longer in the tooth.

I hold no grudges for those who left early and I will always remember the better times.
I wish they would have hung in there as I did as I put aside the bad habits and crimes.
It is that ten seconds before they ended the game I pray no one today will ever see.
Allow the Lord to work the miracle needed in your life to become the best you can be.

OJ-20 years later.

I was in Great Falls wrapping up a degree in college and remarkably behaving myself.
I was holding three jobs and doing school all which kept my whiskey on the shelf.
One of the jobs was a week-end house parent at a safe house for kids society ignores.
Most came covered in lice, hungry as a bear and all the goodness kids have in store.

I was thinking of those little Montana souls I me, reminded by
of all things OJ Simpson.
I was working at the safe house on the day of his slow chase
using the press as a pawn.
I sat in the general area of the house watching my charges as
the others putted about.
What a waste of money OJ was, I was deep in flowers that
which poverty did sprout.

The approach to tending these flowers was to give them the
shelter in the life storm.
A warm bath and soft bed was a luxury to most and sleeping
in cars was the norm.
Our cut off age was sixteen and we only took those who met
the States criteria.
We had no teen age boys as they had a separate house
avoiding sexual hysteria.

I was walking in my garden recalling my visits and time spent
with those poor kids.
The dark secrets they kept to themselves were tucked away-
where their anxiety hid.
My jaw would drop at times at a comment or behavior on
what they thought was right.
It ranged from being sexually suggestive to get their way to
quickly starting a fight.

It was triage of the body and mind as they were interlopers to
these safe walls.
I spent time reading of their activities in protected custody
witnessing social falls.
I have to believe I ended up in that safe place to help because
of my own upbringing.
Butte folk have a place for those hit hardest in life and for the
child who stops singing.

Those months of copper strikes and community wide
hardship changed our Butte lives.
We learned of compassion to fight hardships and the
importance in helping all survive.
There is no added drama needed when feeding and clothing
children was the first task.
Egos were deflated and replaced with the understanding that
there was no need to ask.

I know so many of my Butte friends have gone on to simply
amaze, astound and create.
I like to think that those children I met have ventured on in
life to enjoy the same fate.
I know for a fact that I was able to be helpful on the job
because where I am from.
Who knew that heart break and hard times we had helped
eliminated the fate for some.

It is those hard days on the Richest Hill that made Butte's
people simple and complex.
It is as if they are destined to keep going while walking away
from life's train wrecks.
Most Buttonians feel honored to share their fortune with
others as part of the grand plan.
I for one am grateful for those tough days for it helped me in
life to be a far better man.

Butte Wake.

It has been decades since I have been to a Butte funeral and I
should consider it a blessing.
Mining City family and friends remind me funerals are still
utilized as a large social gathering.
When I think about wakes the first thought is the Butte Irish
and the wakes of the miners.
I was blessed to hear many a good story on the three day
events from my family's old timers.

One of my favorite Irish ditties is entitled "The night that
Paddy Murphy died" all about his wake.
"The Irish got so fucking drunk they still ain't sober yet" is in
the first verse from the song that I take.
It is not just the Irish who hold grand wakes and funerals but
you have to admit they sure do it best.
It can be three to four days of drinking and mourning on
which no one man takes respite or rest.

My family owned the Irish Hotel, the Commercial and it was
full to the rafters with Micks.
In the Nineteen twenties Butte was wide open and
treacherous living was no family picnic.
Only days would go by without the death of an acquaintance
in the mines or on the streets.
Duggan Merrill Dolan the Irish undertakers made sure all
Catholic rules were followed complete.

Many wakes were held at the home as they parked the
deceased in the family's parlor.
For days the friends and family would visit with no need to
hire a professional mourner.
In the kitchen was food but more importantly the drink
needed to celebrate the life.
I have heard stories of the dead being kidnapped much to the
anger of the dead's wife.

The casket would be taken from the house for the trip down
the hill to be buried.
The processions weaved in and out of saloons all the time the
casket was ferried.
Funerals were cancelled for a day while the wake drinking
took priority for all.
"They're dead" said the mourner's, making no deal they
missed the funeral call.

Those days of drinking with a corpse in the Pub are no longer allowed by society's law.
Once again I surmise I lived in the wrong Butte era, wishing I was there to say what I saw.
My days of drinking and toasting have fallen the way of the Butte wake I must admit.
I no longer participate in those Butte wakes and funerals that seemed to never quit.

As with my parents, Butte Funerals are now were friends gather to honor the deceased.
It a gathering of old friends and acquaintances scattered with the winds as living seeds.
I myself hope that some friends get the urge and decide to paint the town in my name.
Scatter some of my ashes on the curb at Maloney's to honor my life that was far from tame.

Put a couple fifths of good Irish whiskey on the bar and let everyone take a good shot.
Tell stories of my life and if I somehow let you down feel free to drink and bitch me out.
You have my permission to take a few days off to make sure I have a great Butte send off.
I will look for you in limbo with the others sinners who like me at the rules we did scoff.

Quintana.

There were six boys in the clan all of us altar boys and
indoctrinated in all that is Catholic.
Mind you there were several other large families made of girls
with a Father so stoic.
For some strange reason or perhaps it was the hands of the
God's that kept it in check.
Why there was never an explosion of marriages had nothing
to do with how the hens peck.

Intertwined like the Irish on the island it was time for new
blood and the clans to expand.
Of course this thought process meant all participants were
good friends with their hands.
If you figured the implication of the last line then you know
there was no interaction.
Yet there was this group of young girls that all the McGinley
boys wanted for fornication.

They were the Quintana girls and I have to admit it is easy to
bring them to mind.
Hispanic Caliente' hot fire with a protective Father who
would kill me if he could find.
Like a pup I would follow them aware more than ever why I
was put on this earth.
To see the Quinta girls in summer dress made many boys
leave the family hearth.

Dark hair captured midnight as if it was their own color
invented in their dreams.
There was no strength any man could hold against what was
held inside their jeans.

You lost your breath and held on tight as they would walk by
and let you know.
As lovely as they were they were just as dangerous as a deep
Butte winter snow.

I hold tightly to those memories when I would knock on
bedroom windows.
Just the chance was all I wanted and from the Quintana girls
they would know.
They were powerful girls and became greater women as our
lives evolved.
I thank God for the Quintana's especially George for the
mystery's solved.

I sit on my porch or perhaps I am fishing and I will think of
those Quintana girls.
They were a sexual fire that drove the boys crazy attempting
to find the pearl.
To this day I am smiling as I think of those Quintana Girls in
all their glory.
How blessed is this Irishman to have such beautiful women in
his life story.

Erts.

I was stopped cold with my evening writing chores as once
again bad news rolls from the Richest Hill.
I will never understand the lottery operated by a deity
deciding whose time it is to be quiet and still.
Many from Butte lived life to the fullest and carried the
Mining City in spirit and with open heart.
Everybody's friend Erts McClafferty fit this description; it was
as if he was born for that part.

I have no idea how Dan got his nickname "Erts" but as with
all Butte handles history is not required.
It was during the time when the Catholic Church decided
operating expenses needed to retire.

Schools were the first to close along with smaller parish clans
and Butte was a melting pot again
North met South, East found West and as with most setbacks
Butte recovered with no real stain.

Since the beginning of the Mining City there has been a Large
Irish presence as a historical fact.
You could swing a dead cat in a Butte bar and hit a dozen
Micks with no need to swing the cat back.
When I started at Central it was my first interactions with
those wild Hill kids who ran as a pack.
As one imagines quick friendships were made, stories were
created for us to laugh and think back.

Erts was easy to pick out in the crowd and I swear to Christ
everyone He knew was a good friend.
There was not a mean bone in our friend as he lived and loved
a good joke right up to the end.
Erts never once turned his back on a friend and in reflection
he lived a very joyful and giving life.
Erts falls into the group of Butte boys who left to early, cut
from us with the reapers unfair knife.

Like many others I thought of our friend on this day, if like me
you wanted just one more chat.
I wish I had spent a little more time with that goofy bastard as
he stuffed his wild hair under his hat.
Erts was quick with a smile and armed the wit of his
ancestors, our pal was no slacker in this life.
Leave it to Erts to put my beliefs to a test as I search for the
reason in this unfair world of rife.

I won't shed a tear but I will shake my head as I recall the
antics of what was a true class clown.
I will remember with a wide smile the last time I ran into Erts
when he was out painting the town.

As with Bubba and the many others we lost far too early I
think it is best we remember their souls.
I believe I will do a good deed in his name and honor for we
all know that's how our buddy Erts rolls.

We will take the walls with us.

I am not sure if you know of this list, it is life events
numerically listed on what brings the most stress.
Of course marriage and the death of a loved one are right at
the top of the fateful list of duress.
There is starting a new job about the middle of the list which
affects everyone on this life stroll.
Back towards the top of this ledger was a high stress activity
that will surely take its deadly toll.

Moving is one of the lives changing events that helps set your
reservation on that cursed early grave.
I find my interest on the subject of moving goes back to my
gypsy radio days when it was music I craved.
The wanderlust lifestyle of decades of traveling made owning
furniture and appliances a pain in the ass.
It was monastic to some as I lived without belongings as I
knew my constant moving left little to amass.

The Good Lord knows I came from a stable household and my
parents enjoyed the rewards you could buy.
There really was no one Butte family I knew of that did not
take pride in their small piece of the American Pie.
The saying "If these walls could talk" applies to rich and poor
alike as all recall sweet memories created.
The saving of the homestead walls and the memories took
new meaning as the Berkley Pit in Butte expanded.

Using the club of Eminent Domain to beat communities into
submission the Company ate away the East Ridge.
There was no standing in the way of progress and mining and
soon we saw houses travelling over a bridge.
The Company paid to relocate households in the small
communities as the consumption rolled on.
Some took the money and built a new residence but it is the
moving of large houses that this tale focuses on.

The Tamietti family took the challenge presented to getting
houses out of the Company's destructive path.
Foundations were knocked down with men swinging sledge
hammers and then it got harder than Chinese math.
The houses were then loaded onto the back of large trucks and
trailers and gently dragged to family's new place.
A number of the houses were moved over those years as
holdouts like McQueen disappeared with not trace.

The production involved in moving a two story house
involved numerous entities to make sure it was done right.
To this day I admire those families who felt tradition and
family were worth saving and well worth the fight.
Many of those houses that were moved are still standing this
day and are a symbol of what makes up Butte Tough.
We all learned valuable lessons from the families and those
who moved mountains to carve a new life in the rough.

The work was back breaking and the logistic of moving would
have had many others throw in the towel.
Those families refused to take "No" for an answer as they got
knocked down and got back up after the fall.
No one person questioned the reasoning of dragging a family
home across the Mining City to start again.
It is that attitude of Can Do that was imbedded in us Butte
Rats as we learned the life lessons to sustain.

The Other Place.

It was the nineteen sixties and America is at war in Vietnam
and in the home land.
Rebellion is at its peak in a disenfranchised youth group with
a valid antiwar stand.
The cracks of corruption ran from San Francisco through the
Rockies into Montana.
Battle lines were drawn with Nixon wrapped in the Flag, the
hippies an old bandanna.

In Butte the Catholic Church was anti war and radical priests
were in the daily news.
Father Finnegan was at the height of his Pastoral power
enlisting his supportive crews.
Finnegan needed a headquarters to reach his masses as he was
limited from the pulpit.
Using contributions and government funds he became and
antiestablishment culprit.

The uniting of a voice for the youth of Butte became the
mission of the leftist Father.
He grabbed up a vacated building and the Humphry Osmond
metamorphism took over.
Music systems were installed and Ina Gada Davida could be
heard playing night and day.
Robert Crumb "Kept Truckin" on the walls as it appeared the
hippy hovel would stay.

My older Brothers and their crews frequented the operation
when it first opened doors.
Bean Bag chairs were scattered about and most members
found their place on the floors.

I was a wee lad during these tumultuous times so my
memories seem to dim and fade.
The youthful attendants suffered mental lapses but from
reefer and acid dropped in shade.

The Youth Center opened and then closed in the blink of the
eye in historic Butte time.
It closed not under scandal, which was waiting in the wings as
a youth home small crime.
Just as it opened with a bump the Other Place shuttered with
a bang but no big surprise.
Butte loves a good parade and protest, but the message of the
sixties held the empty cries.

It was a hell of an effort to drag Butte into a war of the hippies
against the government.
It went over like Mothers Day at an orphanage as it lacked
commitment and sentiment.
The troubles of the sixties found that Butte was not fertile
grounds for experimentation.
Perhaps this never occurred; it never existed and was nothing
more than a hallucination.

Butte never was home to outsider fights and troubles that
spilled on the Montana land.
With copper strikes and children to clothe and feed the
struggles were to close at hand.
Butte versus the world was born out of necessity as Buttonians
knew their own side.
Butte loves a good fight and the sense to choose wisely
without injuring the others pride.

The band wagon of others political stances carry little weight
in the old Mining Camp.
This outlook goes back to the days when Charlie Chaplin was
playing the little tramp.

Get out of Buttes way when it does find a cause for it will
champion it to the very end.
It is the Butte way to get on the right side, with a leftist twist
to make wrong rules bend.

Murphy

Riley my son described Murphy best so there is no need
for a think tank or summit.
Riles said "Murphy is a very cool dog and the best part
is, he doesn't really know it."
Whether it man, a child or in this case a dog great
personalities are welcomed attributes.
It's how we like to remember those we like so much and
offer toasts, cheers and salutes.

Standing next to me for fourteen years Murphy saw a lot
as we chased the elusive work and fish.
I have a many a story on Murphy's antics including
when her turned possums into a dinner dish.
I found him head to head against all interlopers and this
especially applied to all wearing uniforms.
I saw him corner a sheriff and piss off a frightened city
cop delivering snarls and snaps in a storm.

He enjoyed a warm Guinness and as a pup he learned
to knock over the glass to get his fair share.
He ate a wallet full of twenties, puked on a bosses shoe
and walked on without a worry or care.
He was a chick magnet and didn't know it but he
thought the all the pets and free snacks grand.
Murphy came running when out fishing as I called him
into leave by shaking the car keys in hand.

Mandatory pet and damage deposits were waved once
the land lord met his pet tenant face to face.
Murphy had all the tricks down pat, he was never a pest
and being Irish he set his own life pace.

In later years, afternoon naps were the norm and he
slept by preference in the Buick's back seat.
He was run over three times and torn up by pit bulls
but continued on until his trip was complete.

I hate to see the little bugger go, it will be a while until I
quite looking for him laying around.
There is a familiarity and rhythm that can never be
adjusted as our time is finally unwound.
I'll put up his dish and blankets as they are no longer
needed though they take up no room.
One thing is for certain I will always think of Murphy
every time I run the dog hair filled vacuum.

Clothes Line.

When we hear of immigrants these days the majority of
us let our minds set sail to the borders.
Immigrant is associated today with the Hispanic's
entering America despite law and order.
I know more than a few illegals of Mexican descendants
who now live right down the street.
They work hard at tough jobs and in my opinion they
help make my neighborhood complete.

Outside of the changing of signs on the store fronts to
Spanish there is no big sign of the change.
The produce and meat departments have added a
Hispanic flare sort of a Red Neck La Grange.
The signs cater to the newest residents and as with good
there is some bad with the gangs.
The police keep the gang activity down and as with the
all races they maintain tight reigns.

The Hispanics as with all immigrants change the
landscape to make themselves at home.
Since the first arriving nationalities crossed over to Ellis
Island to live here until the death tomb.

I look at New York in the early nineteen hundreds there is link to where Copper is mined
Every neighbor I knew growing up in the Mining City had a pulley powered clothes line.

Dryers were a luxury and with large families there was a need for the washing machine.
The idea of putting clothes in the dryer on a rare hot day would be considered obscene.
Each family placed their lives on display in their back yard to dry in the coppered air.
There were no secrets or humility as the boys finally got to see what the girls wear.

The running of a clothes line signaled to the world that the family was there to stay.
The Montana winters kept their usefulness short as the sun emitted empty rays.
There were the brave souls, the mentally handicapped and newbee's who tried.
They discovered what all of Buttonian's knew as they put pants by the stove to dry.

There were attempts to fly using the clothes line as support leading to a sore spine.
I caught hell from my Dad when I hung firecrackers from our dependable wheeled line.
Clothes Pin guns to shoot wooden matches became the weapon of choice for summer.
The term "Get Clothes Lined" became a reality when not thinking while being a runner.

I am sure there are hold outs that have their line still up and use it in nice weather.
Hang your bedding out to dry with the Montana wind it just does not get any better.

Many a fence line visit began when two neighbors met
while hanging out the clothes.
Perhaps world peace could be found with use of the
clothes line, I'm sure only God knows.

The First of Many.

The story goes I was five years old and running like a
wild banshee around McGinley Manor.
My Dad was saying good bye to some fellow fire fighters
who helped install a basement door.
My Dad with the help of every neighbor, buddy and
fireman dug out our home's basement.
It was a paradise as I could get lost in the confusion
during the project of pouring the cement.

After having a few Lucky Lagers opened with the church
key the fellas left for the night.
As my Dad walked them to the door my brother John
decided to pull a trick to delight.
John poured Clorox into my Dads beer with the hopes
that my Dad would see the joke.
It was a hell of a gamble on John's part as if it failed he
would be in line for a hard poke.

Before my Dad could return I scooped up the beer and
started to pound it down fast.
I had snuck the tasty sips before and experience told me
opportunity is quick to pass.
I had more than a few chugs under my belt when the
burn finally forced me to stop.
Next thing I know is they are forcing me to drink milk
and interrogating John like a cop.

An expensive visit to our second home at the Saint
James Emergency room was called off.
I drank enough milk to dilute the deadly household
cleaner which was deemed enough.

You would think that would have turned me against the drink but that didn't happen.
I turned the other cheek and bent my elbow for years and at the trough I kept lappin'.

Having a sip from Dad's beer was limited to the confines of the family's four walls.
No thought was ever given if they were lighting a fuse to answer to many last calls.
The drink is part of the Irish and is celebrated among many of Butte's ethnic groups.
There is a passage into society associated with drinking and rousing with the troops.

We all remember the sneaking of beers during the holidays and at wedding receptions.
It was a group effort among those underage to get a drink using wiles and deception.
Our parents kindly looked away unless some rookie got louder than the polka band.
Most or all it was a part of life's celebration in Mining Camp held in God's hand.

Not on My Shift Father.

I have known dozens of priests in my life and majority was because of my Father Jack.
Jack dedicated forty years of his life to the parish and he never asked for anything back.
Every priest was welcomed and more than a few were regular visitors in their time.
I learned early that men and women of the cloth were human which was no crime.

My Aunt Rita was a Nun with the order of The Blessed Virgin Mary in the Windy City.
She dedicated her life to teaching in the poorest neighborhood never asking for pity.

When Rita came to Montana the black robes came off as
she smoked and drank a beer.
I was flabbergasted and sworn to secrecy as I learned
that Nuns too enjoy a good "Cheer".

When I consider the amount of clergy Butte had over
the years there was no real trouble.
Parishes in the nation became private brothels with
major litigation to rise from the rubble.
I heard of Native American Children becoming victims to
priest and nuns on the reservation.
Outside of that the cases fall cold and though rumors
persisted of further investigations.

I know not of one whisper or inkling of innuendo that
there was a Wolf among the sheep.
At times corporal punishment got a bit over board and it
was brushed aside without a peep.
There were no frightening rides to Altar Boy picnics and
no secret meetings in the Rectory
The priest's I knew were decent fella's who were miles
away from a perverted trajectory.

A few were odd ducks who carried themselves
awkwardly in public but far from any threat.
A few of them had some very dark secrets yet somehow
there were able to circumvent.
Whatever their activities they were in check as I believe
it was told to the priest recruit.
"Remember Father every day where you are at for they
don't take any trouble in Butte"

The Priests and nuns got away with bloody murder at
the laundries and the orphanage.
In Butte they had a more diverse group in the pews who
had made the mining pilgrimage.

The Church and its representatives were given due respect as they served the Mining City.
I am sure that the spirit of the growing community kept demons away from evil proclivity.

It is one of the stand out traditions of Butte that we will always take our own side.
No matter the opponent of brow beating strike we hung together and took it in stride.
There is no bull shit accepted especially when it comes to kids has always been Buttes rule.
Go against and you will end up alone and banished from every church pew and bar stool.

Wad da yah go by,Buttonian?

If you live in the city of Brotherly Love you take pride in being a Philadelphian.
No matter your roots you call yourself a New Yorker even if you are a Sicilian.
Where I am going is some cities have easy monikers for those who live there.
Other towns I am not sure what to call its citizens, a name that is wise and fare.

Montana seems to have a large supply of city names and what is the citizen label.
Are you a Haverite or Havretonian, Lord only know's about the Anaconda name fable.
Is it Two Doteroinian or perhaps Helenian when discussing the populace of the town?
None of them seem to truly sound correct no matter what you add at the end for sound.

Missoulian sounds quite alright but what in the hell about the folks from Billings?
Bozmanite rings sound and true and yet its neighbor is Butte, a name not thrilling.
I choose to be a Buttonian as it sounds out of earth and flows easily in ones speech.
Butterite sound like a mineral found on the Richest Hill so using it might be a reach.

Being from Butte we've all heard the name rendition done by dropping the e at the end.
Once is OK, twice is an insult, three times almost insures time at the dentist to spend.
The good side is that you have to say where you are from when introducing yourself.
"I'm from Butte" gives others a notice of how you were raised and your mental health.

Even if you don't currently live there it is a life rule that you are always from Butte.
It catches the ears and peaks the interest of the good folks as you explain your roots.
I will always be a Buttonian in my heart, it is from planet Butte where I was born.
Being from Butte I know where I stand, no matter how far from the cloth I'm torn.

Sports Hall of Fame, me?

Many of us return to carrying a blanket as we care for some
thread bare cloth.
It perhaps is a favorite t shirt or hat that we protect from
flames and the moth.
My holy Turin is my T Shirt acknowledging an amazing and
odd placement.
I was inducted with the State Champion Maroons into Sports
Fame encasement.

If you know me at all I worked out every day lifting glasses of
Whiskey and Beer.
I was active in offerings in the Big Sky's outdoors before
raising a glass to cheer.
I play a pretty good game of tennis and enjoy riding my bike
around my hood.
I never played organized sports, quite honestly because I was
never that good.

I enjoyed the camaraderie of many of the school athletes in
and out of school.
I became a Manager for the football teams as they began a
dynasty sport rule.
I only did it for two years before I began working for KXLF-
TV part time.
I had some great road trips with the team while walking along
the sideline.

The State championships reign was epic in the sports world
and is to this day.
It brought school and community together, meaning more
than a game to play.

I took pride in laundering the uniforms of the gladiators and taping ankles.
The guys were very good to me and I count zero arguments or testy rankles.

Fast forward too one of my many journeys to the Mining City to visit the folks.
After a pasty dinner I headed to see my buddy and brother Kevin for a fast toke.
His wife Laura greeted me with her great smile and told me she had a parcel.
She returned in a flash with a wrapped package, its contents were hard to tell.

I opened the package and there was the shirt a gift from the Sport Hall of Fame.
I along with Beans Maunder and Tim Merritt were honored with all the same.
I never expected to be gifted with this recognition and still do not to this day.
I know as I saw first hand the blood and sweat sacrificed by those who did play.

I still have that great T shirt and when I look at all of my travels it is a miracle.
I wear it on no special occasion but when I do I go back with visions empirical.
The long rides on the old Blue Bird bus and unpacking like a traveling band.
The learning of putting the team first and working together began a life plan.

There were a few who knew of my rock and roll escapades and proclaimed fraud.
The better majority are those Butte folks who recognize my effort and applaud.

I myself shake my head in wide wonder as all I did was watch
the teams climb.
It goes to prove that rewards may be delayed but always
arrive in God's time.

The Doghouse

We all heard of men in the doghouse who seek shelter from
the storm named Wife.
They are exiled from their comfortable homes as they weather
the storm of their life.
Some find shelter on the couch of a friend but that is difficult
if the pal is married.
Sleeping in a car in a Butte, Montana winter can leave the
culprit tired and harried.

If the man is a decent bread winner he might find a cheap
hotel to ride out the storm.
Many of these despots had children and mortgages so being
broke is their true norm.
So what is a fella to do when he no longer welcomed at home
for some punishment?
His money is low, he has no where to go so he seeks shelter
charging little or no rent.

If the outcast happened to drink at a Butte bar that had an
upstairs he was in luck.
Not all the saloons had a bed for the wayward soul so many
had to sleep in their truck.
Our family hotel the Commercial was a safe haven for many a
single troubled soul.
There were others scattered on the richest hill where you
could stay with little or no toll.

Above the Milwaukee bar were a set of rooms and apartments used first by rail workers.
They became the home for many tossed out of the home as they were heavy drinkers.
I knew the drill these refuges went through as the daily life of a lush is easy to follow.
Drink in the morning, sleep during the day and close the bar as they drowned the sorrow.

The Honey Moon suites above Jerry's Corner bar gave shelter in the marriage storm.
After a day of heavy drinking it was a stagger up stairs where many a hangover was born.
These were not the best of rooms as they had peeling paint and bugs and mice ruled.
Many were allowed to stay for free as they waited for the wife's temper to be cooled.

I visited a few of these rooms as I returned Butte and would run into a chum on the lamb.
Take my word these were not a penthouse suite and were no bigger that a canned ham.
The bedding was well used by many patrons over the years and was not very clean.
I think it no exaggeration to believe that they could walk alone to the washing machine

They served their purpose, these rooms for the wayward and they saved many a life.
Try sleeping in an unheated room in a Montana winter can make a widow of the wife.
I doubt if the rooms available in the past are offered too today's man tossed on his ear.
One thing is true, if you ended up in one of these rooms it was time to give up the beer.

A Mortician Field Trip.

I was in Fresh man year and the study of ethics was being
kicked about the room.
I am not sure how the conversation circled to death and what
happens before the tomb.
It was thought out by the Christian Brothers and their Minions
the veiled Nuns.
It was a good time to teach children how a full scale mortuary
hums and rums..

There was no better place for the educational experience then
Duggin Merrill Dolan.
Denny would be our tour guide for the afternoon as we were
reminded to be sullen.
I have to admit there were tons of questions that I had about
death and the deceased.
Being Irish I knew from my earliest days that the Mortician
always had a neat crease.

Being the preferred Irish funeral home on the hill I had visited
the building a few times.
It was to say good bye to a favorite aunt or others taken so
young it was a pure crime.
I heard the stories where the Mortuary did their best work
and then the wake moved.
The casket was brought home and place on display as if the
family had turn into druids.

With those stories rattling around my tin head like a marble
that's missing a good chip.
I could only imagine what we were in for as earlier trips I was
guided by my Dad's grip.

Sure enough "Digger" Dolan met the class in the main parlor and explained the rules.
This is a sacred place where God's work is done so there would be no acting like fools.

The embalming room was the first stop; it was as clean and sterile as any operating room.
No great details were offered when appliances were pointed out but one girl did swoon.
We were then corralled to the casket and make up department for a brief touch on attire.
A few jokes about men wearing make up slipped but we know how to properly to expire..

Living in Butte does not give one the edge needed to understand the world Richest Hill.
One has to read and ask questions of the elder's while having Tay by a window sill.
Being Irish and passing along stories I am able to look back and see the future calls.
If you forget the past you can relive it again and again and your life's progress stalls.

I think of the hundreds of souls who lost there last breath retrieving the needed copper.
I see faces in books and imagine their family as they had to fill the undertaker hopper.
My Dad told me the worse wakes in the day was when a closed casket was the rule.
It was a reminder of the death and injury that was under our feet in church and school.

Firebase Murphy.

Wilmington, San Francisco and Missoula, Montana attract
those souls who are the sea glass of life.
Once part of something, now a stand alone entity smoothed
and clouded by sea water and strife.
In the North side of Mootown where the train tracks arrive in
what would be the center of the new city.
It was now a transport destination for the homeless who
always ask for acceptance being full of self pity.

I am the Charles Bukowski of my family tree, I sought out
those bars frequented by hate but lots of laughs.
The down trodden you must remember were once on the top
of a heap at one time some even delegated staffs.
I met engineer named Mac who lived behind a bar but his
days are now destined to wander for beer.
It is that type of dedication to pure self destruction that allows
them the courage not to destroy their fear.

I can write about Fire Base Murphy now because two very
important facts the first being the crew is gone.
The second involves that statute of limitations on the
enterprise they partook in insuring beer and the bong.
It was a cluster of original rooming cabins that was built
around the turn of the century and I never knew the rent.
I would see the occasional former Ranger climb back into his
private bunk house not curious on how his time was spent.

These were spooky Mother Fuckers so I only went around for
business when the sun in the Montana big Sky.
The main room at the front was the office where all sales took
place around a fire burning with coals so alive.

I stayed on the good side with these outlaws for I learned
early in life to sit in the corner while facing the door.
More than a few vouched for my presence in the closed
quarters and in that world you never walked in unsure.

I am quite sure the boys of Fire Base Murphy are long and
gone and scattered as I heard on the line about a bust.
There were rumors of people flipping deals with the
prosecutors to stay away from where steel never rusts.
It is easy imagining their lives got better as they were circling
the drain when I came across them that summer.
For most I have to be realistic in knowing mostly are dear or
incarcerated and if any one made it higher it was a stunner.

From pure experience I have shown you can make the climb
up to being a good person even from the doors of the Firebase
There are those who stay in that life style and being on the
lamb from the law is what they do best in their societal place.
Let's be honest if it was not for the Bad Assess of life we
would have no way to measure out was is good.
After meeting those cold souls and knowing what faced them
later on in their life I decided I no longer could.

It was not the end of my world as it was to some others as I
was always just an interloper in their play house.
I do know for a fact of some doing life in prison while others
died on the streets leaving the world like a mouse.
I was able to walk away from the life style as it takes a great
deal of effort to hold down the position of fuck up.
Not one day goes by that I don't remember those fellas as I
count my daily blessings for shelter and a full cup.

I will remember the porcelain walls, custom wood caskets and
the beeswax candles.
Walking to school more than one thought whose casket they
would hold the handle

Some cities are renowned for their high murder rate or death from a dreaded disease.
In Butte where copper wars flared, the households of Butte took death with quiet ease.

The Bad Ireland,

To start this story with honesty I have to acknowledge that the subject is dead.
He is a lifeless of a bag of hammers and died having to sleep after making the bed.
His last name is Ireland, first name was Dave and he was a Cad and Junkie.
What I write is the truth as I saw it come down in the mid nineteen nineties.

I met Ireland when we both were aiming at the bottom, birds of feather on drugs.
I was a first time visitor to this alley way while Ireland was a regular street thug.
He stole the car of a dying friend one time and his campus visits had a high cost.
Lifting rare books from the U Library was all Dave's gain and society's loss.

It was those smatterings of sociopathic behavior I placed out for you to taste.
I am sure you find them distasteful; Dave was the curly hair in society's toothpaste.
Some are reading and wondering where in the hell is this story winding up.
I have to write to exorcise those vile deeds I need to empty the soul's dirty cup.

It is those goofy bastards that I came across in my life that
keep me toeing the line.
I never forget who I visited with at the Rock Bottom Hotel,
stealing air is the crime.
Like Ireland there were many I knew who rode the crazy train
right off the tracks,
The commitment to evil and self destruction is a life that is not
fully unpacked.

I am no better than those cats and kittens of who I scribe about
in simple prose.
The only difference was I found moral boundaries in their
world of I suppose.
Being born in Butte I have learned to forgive the drinker and
the side stepper.
It is how any good bartender would deal with junkies and
other of life's lepers.

I have to recall those tough times on a regular basis especially
when it is good.
No better way to compare today's blessings to the time when
nothing stood.
I recall but I will never revisit as I am a bit older and wiser in
my approach.
I keep it between the lines and no longer utilize Bukowski as
my Life Coach.

Meaderville Spaghetti.

Being Irish and feeding a hurling team my parents did
everything on a grand scale.
Feeding the boy's, large portions were prepared with boiling
in a pot as big as a pail.
Outside of Pasties the Irish pallet can be a bit bland to those
with spicy ethnic tastes.
Butte Gatherings were such a treat for the Cornucopia of food
I shoveled into my face.

Our family gatherings were great but mostly all of the same
fare though still not bland.
It was the trips to McQueen and other locations where the
feasting became quite grand.
Grand Ma Minnie Uggetti's ravioli was hand made with a
recipe a hundred years old.
It was those morsels of how the other half lived that showed
we were in the dietary cold.

Many different groups adopted recipes to be used on Sunday
for the weekend feast.
Butte families adopted a Meaderville Spagehetti,each a poor
knockoff to say the least.
Don't get me wrong for even the poorest attempts to copy the
dish always tasted the best.
It was the true recipes from the finer eateries in Meaderville
for which there is no contest.

All claimed the name of Meaderville's creation that was
imported to the Mining Camp.
It was the new taste for the Irish miners who ate their pasties
in the mines by a head lamp.

There was a great pride allowed for the creators of the dish that put all others aside.
The delicate taste enraptured all those took part and soon the recipe took a short ride.

Soon Dublin Gulch and Walkerville brought the taste of Italy into their home kitchens
No matter the efforts and best attempts by all the cooks they found themselves reaching.
The attempts were not frugal as the meal fed the Copper City and its diverse crowd.
It is that sharing of life's pleasures and tough times that makes this Irishman Butte Proud.

A Pork Chop In Every Glass.

In the Mining community support systems are in place for whatever the day brings.
It can range from a Doctor who comes in a moments notice to set a broken wing.
There was the beloved priest who visits the family after the loss of a family member.
We can not forget the neighbors who prepared funeral meals always to remember.

Friends are at the front of the line when it comes to a family getting through the tough.
They clear the path of any obstacles or offering a shoulder to lean on when it got rough.
There are the tax paid departments that protect the homes against burglars and fire.
The support of all comes together to help all keep moving forward with life's desire.

The medical field has put together more damaged folks so that they can enjoy life.
There was no replacing of home care delivered by the much loved Mom and Wife.
Friends are always there to visit during the times when one needs to sort it all out.
We learned early in Butte that being there for one another was what this life is about.

With all these support systems in place one wonders how some needy can slip by.
We wonder how they never received attention as they wandered under the Big Sky.
Some of these lads have chosen that solitary life and many of them hit hard the drink
Many wonder how they are able to survive and how they handle life's unseen kinks.

The rationalization these men use to validate their lives is a question mark to most.
A man is destroying his life with Satan's nectar; it's a miracle they are not yet a ghost.
It is not just the men under the bridge who live this life of hard drinking all day long.
One thing I have learned is that many believe that this is their life's repeating song.

I have heard many reason and a few excuses on how a heavy drinker justifies the act.
Drinking shots with beer chasers for breakfast make it hard to keep their job intact.
One of the best lines I heard spoken in the Butte bars to justify the consumption.
"There's a pork Chop in every glass" rationalizing drink over a meal of nutrition.

Although said with a lilt there was some truth especially
when drinking a Guinness.
Some nutrition is found in the elixir of the monks though the
diet can be heinous.
It has been said that an Irish seven course meal is a six pack
and well cooked potato.
It is the rationalization of life's survival being found under the
bar signs that glow

More than a few times I have heard this reasoning delivered
with jest but some truth.
We are talking about men who used whiskey for a pain killer
to deaden an angry tooth.
It starts out with a couple beers after work as the gathered to
shake of the dust of the job.
With no meal to balance the intake of beer it takes a few hours
to become a drunken slob.

In my travels I came across bars happy hours where fine food
is put out for the spread.
I have seen pretzels and peanuts as old as dust that drunken
patrons considered well fed.
No matter the reasoning we all know the truth that drinking
for meals is a bad thought.
It begins innocently but soon takes the man ransom as in the
drinking web he is caught.

True there is some nutrition in beer but as the main staple it
falls short for one's needs.
No matter the joking the ugly truth comes to light as the
drinker sows destructions seeds.
The joking and laughter that goes with a good drink takes a
back seat to the day drinking.
And the end of the journey they look at a life wasted and
wonder what was I thinking.

Mom the General Contractor.

It has been awhile since I visited the McGinley Manor in the center of the city.
It's a brick home that was headquarters for activities for both adults and kiddies.
When my parents bought the house it was a fixer upper project to say the least.
My Mom and Dad did turn it around and paid off the mortgage to the bank beast.

If you do any type of project around the house the chances are good for a grand mess.
Imagine if you will painting a wall with numerous children in various stages of undress.
There are visitors in and out of the house as you slap paint and cook the family dinner.
You have three in school and three under feet who are trying to drink the paint thinner.

The renovations took place under watchful eyes of parents to keep kids from harm.
There was painting and hanging paneling all done without sending out an alarm.
The holidays continued while my Dad and friends dug out a basement to expand.
It's a miracle what they accomplished while raising the clan on this patch of land.

There were a few paint jobs on the brick exterior and I recall my Dad replacing the roof.
The roof projects were done while he worked as a fireman, my Dad was far from aloof

With all the projects I do not recall one argument as the task
had them joined at the hip.
I am sure there were some minor disagreements but there
never was a curse word to slip.

I took it for granted, yet as I think of this dynamic today I take
a special look at Mother.
She was not a believer of having bells and whistles but man
she could run a wood sander.
Her uniform of the day was always colorful and had simple
prints and bright vivid colors.
She dressed for her day knowing that the world would bring
hard duty far from stellar.

As with all the neighborhood mothers the work days were fun
and full of surprises
We children only added to the chaos as the Moms dealt with
constructions crisis.
New flooring was put down in the blink of an eye as a
plumbing upgrade occurred.
I admire how they improved our lifes while making sure the
stew pot got stirred.

I keep the attitude of improving my surroundings and to leave
every place a bit better.
It is one of the lessons I am so grateful for, the ability to take
on construction unfettered.
I learned as much from my Mom as I did with my Dad when
it comes down to a remodel.
You have to admire any woman who can handle power tools
better than a cooking ladle.

Nope, not here.

No matter the frivolity and fun that was had, there is always
tomorrow morn.
It is the day after a night of good drinking when I wish I had
never been born.
I crawl out of bed shaking off the cobwebs that have grown on
my pickled brain.
I begin the ritual of recalling the night while thinking a gun
might end this pain.

The first act of recovery is to assess ones losses and a good
place to start is with cash.
The pants I wore weigh five pounds more, coins the
remainder of the high dollar stash.
I realize the money I had saved for a new raft to float is now
deep in another's pocket.
I look out the window and realize that my car is not in the
place where I usually park it.

"Sonofabitch" is the muttered curse as I grabbed coffee and
recall the night's activities.
This is going to take a while as I revisit the night, well aware
of my own proclivities.
I need to find my wingman and fast; I know that he was a
witness to the Monster ball.
Calling his house his Dad say's he never made it home as my
jaw slowly begins to fall.

Knowing I am going to get bitched out big time, I go to the
kitchen to borrow a car.
Dad shakes his head as he tosses his set, telling me to hurry
up and don't go too far.

Looking through my pockets for clues I come across a pull tab turning on a switch.
I had breakfast at the M&M which a good place to start to deal with this mind itch.

I made a few circles in the uptown area in case to the M&M I had decided to walk.
My mind begins to show some cognition coming through, while to myself I did talk.
Still no sign of my chariot so off to the Flats, I need to expand this widening search.
It was a wild night for sure so God only knows on what barstools I decided to perch.

Charlie Judd's and a visit with Mike took place and they have a huge parking lot.
Chances are good that the car would be there, and that became a wrong thought.
The only car in the lot was a wrecked Buick as it sat by itself watching the wall.
I continue the search down Utah and Arizona for I can not remember the last call.

It was not at the Deluxe but I do recall being there having a few and shooting dice.
It is time to hit Harrison Avenue and Sparky's Lounge hoping this would suffice.
Sure enough there sits the focus of my search, thankfully it has not one scratch.
I get out and open up the door and the smell was something a pirate ship could match.

There was half eaten food and spilled drinks on the floor board making a terrible stain.
There in the back seat is my wingman sleeping one off about to experience my head pain.

With a wale he acts as if he has amnesia asking me who, what, when, where, and why.
I wait as he exorcizes his morning demons telling me his regrets and his own wish to die.

I give him my keys and I tell him to take my car home and to pick me up a bit later.
A shower will help and perhaps a few Bloody Mary's will be a hang over eliminator,
My buddy tells me it sounds like a plan to get together and piece together last night.
After we go looking for his car that he too lost, some place on that Butte Saturday night.

She was all Irish

I need to put one thing on the table to get it out of the way, to deal with an issue.
I am sure I need to look at this straight and honestly with no need for a tissue.
My friend Terri Monahan was stuck with a Butte nick name that really had no place.
Dubbed with a nick name is not all good and we wish they were gone with no trace.

That out of the way I now look at my friend Terri's remarkable life and all she gave.
I know without knowing and feel the trace of her goodness in the lives that she saved.
When I read that she left the confines of earth my first thought was of her great laugh and smile.
It was easy to put Terri's smile in my mind's eye and her laughter that could be heard for a mile.

I remember Terri when in attendance at Butte Central and there was no bigger Maroon Fan.
She cheered all her brothers on in athletics as well as all the other players out of the Monahan Clan.
She carried that spirit and love for the game of a good life with her and always close to her heart.
I can attempt to list of all the good about Terri but there are too many and I know not where to start.

So I will close again on what was most prevalent about my friend as I try to understand this loss.
I then think about Terri entering the grand gates of heaven telling Saint Peter she's the new boss.
That smile that could bring the clouds to earth and a laugh that will echo forever on our souls.
With Terri passing I am reminded to stoke the fires of all my friendships with my treasured coals.

Aqua Velva Stingers, no ice.

When it comes to making home made brew I have tasted some of the grandest.
I have also sampled the bottom of the barrel all with curiosity and self interest.
These include the tapping of red wine in a buddy's basement before a dance.
We tipped mason jars of fruited brandy snuck out with out a parents glance

I recall drinking McQueen Grappa in flaming shots that set a table on fire.
Oh there were bad batches that would be better used to start a funeral pyre.

Sweet wine that turned to vinegary poison was spat out with
vile disgust.
When not used for drinking some were poured on metal to
remove rust.

I have been offered some unknown elixir that was
questionable in origin.
Drinking of alcohol that borders on rocket fuel can destroy
man's organs.
There were Native Americans in the Walkerville area that had
it quite bad.
My Mom told me of them drinking Aqua Velvet after shave,
so damn sad.

I was doing a week end jail stint in Great Falls and witnessed
jail hootch.
The organization and pooling of supplies, all designed to
screw the pooch.
They had varied recipes involving Lysol as the source of the
needed juice.
They pounded it down and got rowdy as hell as they got loose
as a caboose.

The other brewing crew used deodorant and squeezed the
wax in a shirt.
The juice of Mennen was collected from many all while being
on alert.
It was high concentration and mixed with juice before it was
consumed.
Before long they too were drunk as the trouble blossomed and
bloomed.

I have seen film of bears getting ripped up on corn fermented
in the sun.
It seems most creatures have found intoxication as the fun
place to run.

Most times in social settings it is polite to sit back and knock down a few.
When you resort to drinking detergent the drinking habit is due for review.

My Uncle Eddy was a big drinker and in tough times he found the way.
They poured grain alcohol through a loaf of bread to keep poison at bay.
The drink was called "Smoke" and it was used often when money was tight.
It is just another example of ingenuity and need to get through a tough night.

They say that natural elements of intoxication are best when left alone.
The introduction of man to modify and change always changes the tone.
I am not recommending a thing; your life is yours to do with as you wish.
Just keep it as natural as possible and avoid all coming from a Petri dish.

As I did on that very long week end, I watched and learned of extremes.
I count my blessings I never shot those white waters of drunken streams.
The lesson I took away with me to contemplate is a mix from what I saw.
No matter if it is Martini's or Aftershave it is all hair of the dog's paw.

Ears Knows.

I am one of those lads who has the face of Ireland carved into
my Irish head.
This analogy carry's merit as we look at faces and how they
are often read.
We who own the heritage of a hard living race absorb that face
of that land.
Changes are glacial but as time moves on our features become
less bland.

Let us look first at the honker, the nose, the compass of every
nationality.
As with Pinocchio but with out the lying, it grows bigger
exponentially.
It becomes sharp as a hook or in the Irish case as bulbous as a
mountain.
As the face withers in the nose grows into a personal
memorial fountain.

The pork chop ears are the biggest fear as Dumbo gets a run
for the show.
In high wind rocks are carried in pockets to avoid a ride as the
winds blow.
It size might be needed as hearing diminishes and all sound
falters away.
No matter the size they are the frame of the land that holds no
time at bay.

The window to the soul, the eyes have it when separating all
from the rest.
The twinkle of the Irish to the sultry Mediterranean distinctive
lives at best.

I recognize eyes before the features of the face as they are the measure of life.
They capture our spirit and our heritage reflecting all of the love and the strife.

The second chin holds the baggage of our life as the jowls begin to set loose.
Heredity plays out its hand as each mug develops from a life war with no truce.
It is not only the members of the Emerald Isle who reflect the face of the land.
I can pick out a Sicilian nose as easy as the life lines on a laborer's harden hand.

I see the photographs of distant family and I recognize a lost Uncle or Aunt.
No matter the years the reflection of family smolders in the friendly haunt.
No matter how I change and wither in body my face will continue to change.
The history of life and habits good and bad all contribute as features rearrange.

I have grown comfortable with this mug as I hope you have with what was given.
No nips and tucks as I have earned the wrinkles and lines of a life hard driven.
I will recount the stories of the scars and broken noses as I move into my December.
The face is the journal of our lives open for all to read and hopefully to remember.

Mining City Pants.

I am not what you would call a clothes horse, I am actually more of and ass.
I find daily comfort in my ten year old jeans, formal wear it would never pass.
Give me a used golf shirt from Goodwill worn earlier by some retired banker.
My garb for rambling about the forest but at a wedding it could infuse ranker.

Going to a Catholic School I wore Salt and Pepper britches as the day uniform
After school attire was composed of hand me downs acquired in the perfect storm.
My haberdasher was my Mother well versed with scissors and her Singer machine.
Color co-ordination or matching was no priority, nor was being neat, tidy and clean.

When days are filled with exploring the industrial world clothes will get destroyed.
It is those full days of life in Butte youth that gave me courage to not dodge or avoid.
I was not encouraged to be tough on my pants but I never got in trouble for doing so.
I was allowed to be boy and learned what the basics were and what brings me true joy.

I had what were called my good clothes, kind of like Opie Taylors go to church pants.
They were never worn after school or for play hours or God did I hear my Dad rant.

Being the youngest of six boys and no sisters around fashion was not of a concern.
It was that early division of my pants that gave me valuable lessons to live and learn.

The first thing I learned is that other Butte kids had the same clothing and dress rule.
It was the rare freak who could dress to the nines to play kick the can after school.
Clothes were not important to measure my station in life and my every day existence.
All pants had a purpose but had nothing to do with character or what is social stance.

Oh there were times I was embarrassed of my clothes, all due to my wrong thinking.
It was in those times I learned about the book and the cover and what is truly revealing.
Being in the same boat as the others on the street we all kept our Butte fashion in check.,
I was taught how to me how dressing nice for a wake or wedding was a sign of respect.

I salute my meager wardrobe and give my worn tweeds a salute on this beautiful fall day.
I still have nice pants I have not worn in a long while and it is on the hanger they stay.
If have to put nice pants on any more it is to bury a friend and not to dance in the night.
I will stick with my worn jeans and golf shirts as my uniform to do battle in the life fight.

Those who love fashion and wear all the best I thank you for the color gifted to the world.
If being condescending is your only accessory, step back as my Irish becomes unfurled.
We know not what journey the legs in those torn jeans have taken throughout the day.
Keep in mind those worn out knees in my pants are because they stopped to kneel and pray.

Stool Crazy.

I listen to and have read many stories about being stuck in a company town.
The destiny to be a steel worker or a miner for life can create a serious frown.
To climb into a machine that hurtles you underground to make another man rich.
For most it is the hand life has dealt and fuel for the many that moan and bitch.

As my father before me and his father too it can be all that fills a life short dream.
To buck against this life choice is for those brave who rage against the machine.
The scholastics pulled their act together and studied hard to escape this old life.
They found an opening from being stuck in a job unable to care for child and wife.

Some do not see the downfall of a limited experience and are content as a clam.
I admire those who can make the best of their life even with a limited life plan.

The pulling of an honest shift and building a family home is not my target here.
It is the efforts of the older citizenry offering an escape plan is what I do cheer.

If you were limited in scholastic abilities it seems that a Company job was good.
It offered stability and decent living for a family in a Butte mining neighborhood.
Many a Dad would reach out to his boss to help a family member land a good job.
Closing windows to the world it opened local doors so none felt they were robbed.

With higher education the Butte Schools offered the initial plans to make the break.
It was the greatest generation who wanted more for their kids in their own life's stake.
Plans were put in place to advance the horizons of the children they loved from start.
It began with educational tools so they did not end up in jobs of no ending or start.

For the Butte girls it was Home Economics so they could learn how to run a house.
They were ferried to Webster Garfield to attend the classes on how to sew a blouse.
For the boys the classes were designed to work with their hands and build a bench.
It involved mechanical drawing and working with wood and learning to use a wrench.

When I attended I had Mr. McDonald who somehow kept us all in a straight line.
We built a foot stool that had little use at home but most turned out rather fine.
The basics of life were taught to us as we learned to work and complete a task.
All were held equal as we presented useless gifts to our parents to own and bask.

The footstools in our house all ended up in the garbage as they offered little use.
Though well constructed they would never last long with six boys swinging abuse.
I speak not for the girl's projects but I know their life lessons were taught as well.
We all looked at the possibilities outside of the mining camp as the job walls fell.

These days are full of powerful computers and phones to locate our own lost asses.
I believe this next generation would benefit from taking a few of the manual classes.
I look back to those foot stools and I can trace my interest in using my hands to build.
The small projects of creation are inspiration on how to keep my simple mind filled.

Now there will be those who call me a stodgier and believe I am hopelessly lost in time.
I won't disagree as I embrace the old school ways committing a small anti-social crime.
I admire the technology and all the fine gadgets but to forget this message I am remiss.
Remember youth's lessons and the sacrifices of Butte parents all for their children's bliss.

Kearney.

It is a rare occurrence in Butte when you have to reach out and ask for some help.
Butte neighbors and ones family answer the alarm before a kicked dog can yelp.
Whether a Father and Husband were lost to the Hill the Butte community steps up.
I had not mean tragedy as the only support we help out a guy well into his cup.

I could be a couple of bucks until pay day or a bag of groceries left on the porch.
Butte people do the best to help others and I work to carry that spirited torch.
Clothes were shared and gatherings took place to make sure the other survived.
It is how Butte has lived and it is what makes it continue to invent honest pride.

When I first launched my books I received bad advice from a publishing house.
I pulled back, reflected and realized they were the fat cat and I was the mouse.
I looked to my past as I knew what I needed for my future was waiting there.
I looked to my mentors and those who know better eliminating my despair.

When writing about Butte I reached out to Pat Kearney, historian extraordinaire.
If any one knew how to skin this cat quickly Pat would have the time to spare.

Kearney got right back to me in a matter of a day even though
time had tolled.
We picked up on our friendship as if it was just yesterday,
that is how Pat rolled.

He gave me sound advice as I knew he would and offered his
assistance for later.
My first book hit the market and Pat was of the first to buy it,
a friendly instigator.
There are some great guys who Butte looses early and it is
hard to figure it out.
Meaner souls should be taken before Pat but that is not what
Pat and Butte are about.

Pat was born into Butte and knew he needed to stay a he
worked for his home town.
Nor the strikes or tough times stopped Kearney from getting a
smile from a frown.
I tip my hat to Paddy, he was a hell of a guy who did wonders
for the mining camp.
He was a true Butte lad, a friend to the many and Buttes
favorite sporting champ

Mairissa.

I have never been blessed by the Pope and never shook hands
with a standing president.
I have walked the halls of power in my career days seeing
how good laws make a dent.
I have met so many good people that inspire and set a
powerful goal for all to reach for.
It is the blessing that they make a huge difference before
God's closing of their life's door.

I admire those who live the great life and it is second nature that they make a change.
What makes this undertaking of such responsibility forces my thoughts to rearrange?
I do not believe they know the influence they possess and the gift they freely give away.
It is as simple a smile or an encouraging word that enlightens other's lives every day.

I read the testimonials others give in these great individuals with all of their heart.
When I am surmising the gifts these great souls offer I find no difficulty how to start.
It is the interpretation of their place in this world is where I find a very small problem.
They are the flowers of our life as I try to describe from where the greatness stems.

Butte's Mairissa Peoples is the focus of this small attempt to capture her glory.
The good people she encouraged with a never ending smile is the basis of this story.
I know the first generation of Mairissa's clan as her grandfather was a family friend.
It is easy to understand the influence they had on Marrisia until her day's very end.

This powerful child took the desperation of disease and made it a source of her power.
The simple words of encouragement and her demonstration of faith flowed every hour.
I watched at a distance and read of her accomplishments in complete admiration.
There is no understanding why she left us so early when greatness was her destination.

I cannot question the workings and operations of this world of
which we are visitors.
I do know that when Marrissa walked this earth she was a
precious gift of the Creator.
It is so difficult to fathom why this special and engaging girl
enjoyed so little time.
I know that her message of love and support remains forever
and in eternity sublime.

150
My Grandfather Mike was the proud owner of only one leg,
but it is heart I admire.
The lace curtain to the past of this Irish barman makes me
wish I had seen it transpire.
I believe the secrets have to deal with how he got him fortune
so early to build a hotel.
Nineteen years old and fresh off the boat, how he built it is a
story no one would tell.

His is but one of Buttes great stories that have taken place in
the Rockies Mountain walls.
This mining camp invented by mad visions bankrolled the
cluttered of the odd sprawl.
His ways with a buck fit in well in Buttes bust and he and
other immigrants faired well.
What I would give to hear how he found Butte riches walking
away from Ireland's hell.

Guns in Butte were all part of recipe of settling all disputes
and some questions dealt out.
An Elk on the table with family and friends at hunt camp is
what its Butte's all about.
There were more than a few chapters where a pistol settled
card debts and the tough odds.
Stray lads took their own lives but I don't judge, I leave that to
them and their Gods.

Some said the old girl would never see eighty let alone a solid
yard and a half.
There were a few times a wake was held for Butte, as they
flew the flags half staff.
Many close calls that had the strength of ten winters in sealing
Butte in its timed place.
The hearty men who created her allowed the Rockies to
landscape their leathered face.

What is chaos with out law and order, what is the life if has
not fireworks and pain.
Black powder blew a hole in the mountain where copper
coursed deep in alls veins.
Screaming sirens alerted the citizens of the changing of shifts
of the mole life below.
Men gave their lives for what was growing on the surface as
Butte began to grow.

The city hit six figures in population some thought it to be the
next San Francisco.
Tall buildings were erected and the landscape expanded in
spite of winter snow.
The delicacies of fancy living found their way to the Copper
City on Daly's hill.
The rich got richer as the mine went deeper and many a
miner's blood did spill.

The growth enjoyed by many started to whither in the labor
strikes took a toll.
The disputes took violence by the hand as the strikes grew like
the fire of coal.
Families decided to evade the troubles and packed to leave the
Mining City.
Those who stayed received the support of the community
with out enduring pity.

The Berkley pit was deemed to be empty of the minerals that brought all about.
The pumps were turned off, the water began filling with water the color of stout.
Abandoned like an orphan from most other cities it seemed Butte has seen her last.
It was then decided that there was another bit of wealth in embracing Butte's past.

The turn around was not easy for Butte but nothing ever was easy for this place.
The damage of winters stole the youth from the buildings as they fell to disgrace.
The roofs of strong shelter in the past now fell onto the floors under times weight.
Most would have given up the ghost but Butte pulled together to make a new fate.

The challenges were not easy but true Butte leaders came to the front of the pack.
A community chased away the disappointment in a new economic growth attack.
Some said it was too late for the jewels of the city had been taken to never return.
True to Butte fortunes and belief in the toughness would light the embers to burn.

Soon Saint Paddy's day gave birth to tourism and music festivals filled the sky.
I see these festivities and realized that fine Butte was ready for another bold try.
The generations of over coming adversity had taken shape in brave new form.
Butte had learned that no matter the trouble there would be calm after the storm.

Butte sits today on the top of the heap, building a new future on the tailings of old.
With genuine appeal throngs now go to this city created by the brave and the bold.
Butte will see two hundred, I believe it will and then some as the winters blow down.
No matter the outlook of those outside, Butte, she will always be Montana's crown.

Slan, Beir bua agus bannacht. Padraíg Magfhionnghanle

(Bear Victory and Blessing!   Patrick McGinley)

Made in United States
Orlando, FL
10 April 2022

16677486R00046